Lefthanded
Soldiers

by Gary Eby

Published by
www.YourSuccessStore.com

Distributed by
www.YourSuccessStore.com
2835 Exchange Boulevard
Suite 200
Southlake, Texas 76092
(877)-929-0439

Lefthanded Soldiers/Gary Eby

ISBN: 13: 978-1-4243-3040-9

Printed in The United States of America

Dedication

Dedicated to all of those who have been wounded in life, whether physically, emotionally, spiritually, or financially and yet, against all odds, have risen from the devastation to become a champion!

Acknowledgements

With a grateful heart I'd like to acknowledge the hundreds of trainers, speakers, motivators, philosophers, ministers and teachers I've been blessed to sit under in my lifetime. From their live meetings, cassettes, CDs, emails and books I've heard and read, thousands of quotes, illustrations and stories, that over the years I've adapted and used again and again. It is impossible, in most cases, to remember the origin. So, I freely acknowledge that the biggest part of what I know, what I have to share, and who I am is because the providential grace of God allowed these great men and women to pour their gifts into my life.

I also humbly acknowledge that in these illustrations, and even in my personal stories and testimonials, that the passage of time may occasionally have a way of filling in the blank spots of our memory, but still allows for the fundamental life-changing truths to stay unaltered.

And without fail, I'd like to acknowledge the support, wisdom and faithfulness of my wife and children who continually teach me by their life's example. They are my heroes.

What Others Are Saying

"I'd like to thank the person responsible for inviting Gary to speak at our company today. And, I want you to make sure that you are responsible for inviting him back! And ... when you do, I absolutely want you to make sure that I'm in town to hear him! Gary's message today was wonderful. It was both powerful and eloquent. His words were motivational ... but more importantly ... they were inspirational!"

Zig Ziglar
Motivational Speaker

"Gary Eby is a powerful speaker. He moved me when he said, 'You can't have a testimony without a test'. That is so true. As a sportscaster I see this all the time with young coaches and players. Even veterans have to deal with tests. I saw Gary Eby speak last year and I bought his CD program, 'Power Principles for Peak Performance'. They are must haves for me. They get me motivated for work."

Newy Scruggs
Sportscaster, NBC Universal, KXAS

"I have the opportunity to work with some of the great speakers out there... Jim Rohn, Denis Waitley, Chris Widener... and now Gary Eby. Gary's full of vision, integrity ... and he's diligent about what he does ... he makes a connection with the audience... and he'll make a difference for you."

Kyle Wilson
President, Jim Rohn International

continued on page 127

Lefthanded Soldiers

Contents

Chapter One
The Day of Battle

As I awoke, I quickly became aware of the eerie quietness that was hovering over the camp. The sound of my own breathing was all I could hear. I was relieved when I finally heard, the gentle "cooing" of the morning doves. Soon, the ever present locust came to life and joined this morning chorus. They began to sing their greetings, sending out a secret code that only they could understand. A gentle breeze began to blow causing the door flaps of my tent to rustle just enough to keep me from going back to sleep.

The sweet smell of freshly brewed coffee began to drift through the crisp morning air. I began to pick up the faint aroma of breakfast! The thought of a crushed, sweet fig spread across the top of a freshly baked bread cake, caused me to smile! I've always loved to eat breakfast while watching the sunrise. This ethereal, sensory combination stirred me just enough to at least "try" to wipe the cobwebs from my mind and the crust from the corners of my eyes.

So, just as I had done hundreds of times before, I let out an earth shaking yell. "I'm alive!" It was my tradition. I loved to greet the morning at the top of my lungs. I was serving notice to the world that I was alive! I threw off my blankets, quickly dressed, and walked barefoot across the field. The last remnants of the morning dew not only washed my feet, but it also washed whatever was left of sleep completely out of my mind.

I joined my fellow soldiers as we met in small groups and broke bread together. We came from hundreds of villages. Each of us had our own dreams. We all had lives to return to. But, for now, this was our life. Ours was a life of sacrifice, danger and perils. But it was also a life of nobility, honor, and glory. My name is Jason, and I'm a soldier. A Lefthanded Soldier. Soon, the thoughts of breakfast turned into thoughts of battle. The coming events of the day began to dominate my thoughts. Today was the day. The day of battle!

Our army was encamped in the Cedron Valley. We were surrounded by the moonlit hills of Judea. The sunrise had not yet made its appearance, but, none the less, I quickly became aware of the excitement and anticipation that was already building throughout our camp. Today was the day! This was no time for laziness! The enemy was not sleeping in. The enemy was not dwelling on the past or longing for the future. The enemy was preparing for the day at hand! To a soldier "today" was always the most important day!

It wasn't long before the gentle "cooing" of the morning doves had been replaced by the sounds of a great army in motion. With each passing minute the necessity for preparation was gaining momentum. Men were starting to move in every direction. The armaments of battle were all being assembled. The blacksmiths were taking all the swords in hand and making sure they were sharp and well oiled. Shields were polished, banners were raised, and standards were unfurled.

My comrades and I began to equip ourselves for battle. First, we put on our corselets made of either leather or quilted fabric. Then we put on our breastplates to cover and protect our hearts. Next came our shoes and leggings. These protected our feet and legs. Our loins were covered to protect our manhood. We all had our own special helmet made for us personally. We also carried a great frontal shield or a smaller shield called a buckler. The goal was to protect every area of our body, as much as possible. This preparation was almost ritualistic. We were not only preparing our bodies, we were preparing our minds. Most of the battle is won hours before the engagement!

By now, the sun was fully risen. The highly polished metals glistened in the morning light as the troops began to assemble. By tens, by hundreds, by thousands, we fell into rank. We all had a spot. I was in mine! Every man a spear, every man a shield, every man a sword. But, none of these for me, I was a Lefthanded Soldier!

Chapter Two
Wounded

I was part of a special elite unit. We were called "Lefthanded Soldiers." In the battle that day we would not use a sword. We would not carry a spear or other similar tools of battle. I, and six hundred and ninety - nine of my closest friends, would only carry a sling!

And yet ,we, along with our comrades, would still go into battle!

What a picture! Seven hundred Lefthanded Soldiers, carrying only a sling, all going into battle.

How absurd! To be quite honest, when our unit was first formed, we were often laughed at. Sometimes when we first approached the enemy they laughed us to scorn. They wondered, " what kind of a joke was this?" They did not laugh for long!

I assure you, we were not a laughing matter. We were a highly trained, specially selected elite band of soldiers!

Each one of us had been "hand" chosen. All for a very special reason. History would write of us that we were seven hundred men, chosen men, lefthanded men, who could sling a stone at a hair breath, and not miss!

So, how did this unusual band of soldiers that I was a part of come about? What was our genesis? Why "lefthanded" soldiers?

Let me explain. I have learned that none of us would be where we are today unless we had gone through each and every event of our life. We are a composite of our life experiences. Good, bad, indifferent--we are who we are, in large part, because of our life experiences.

Our victories have helped mold us. Our adversities have helped build us. Our experiences, whether terrific or tragic have made eternal deposits in our mindset. We are who we are because of where we've been and what we've been through. These events, though, do not determine our destiny. How we deal with them does!

Today I am a soldier ready to protect and defend that which is dear to me. I am ready and willing! That was not always the case.

It wasn't that long ago that I was sitting at home. I was depressed, I was disillusioned, and I was discouraged.

I was hopeless.

After years of glorious military service, I had suffered a severe, career ending injury. I was a master swordsman. I was a leader of great men on the field of battle. But, after a severe injury to my right arm, I could no longer use a sword. My arm had been severed just below the elbow. It was not an uncommon injury. Since almost my entire body was covered and protected, the most vulnerable spot was my fighting arm. It was exposed, so it was vulnerable. In fact, most of the nonfatal wounds in battle were to the right arm since we, like all men, were predominately right handed.

It was a part of our history. In hand to hand combat, hands were lost, tendons were cut, and parts of arms were severed. The regrettable thing is that when your army survives with a sword and a spear and you cannot use those weapons any longer, you are relegated to menial tasks...or retirement.

And when you are a warrior, retirement is better than a life filled with meaningless tasks and watching the battle from afar. It's far less painful to just fade away!

So, through the years, hundreds of wounded warriors just like me, from generals to captains to common foot soldiers, had taken the longest walk of their lives--the walk home.

We felt we were relegated to a life of memories, disappointment, and sometimes great bitterness.

It wasn't fair. We had given our lives for a great cause. We had fought for what we believed in! And now, because we had been wounded, it seemed to some that we were no longer useful! We had gladly given our blood, sweat and tears and now it seemed as though our lives were over! We'd gone from feeling like heroes to feeling like zeros! It just wasn't fair!

One thing made it worse. The sword that had cut off my arm had also severed my ability to move on with my life. My life had become a continual stream of "what if's."

Chapter Three
Thank God For Leaders

But, then one day something amazing happened. The day had started off like all others. After a fitful night of tossing and turning I woke up in a bad mood. I was grumbling about anything and everything. Ruth, my wife of fourteen years had just about reached her wit's end. I had tested her once optimistic demeanor to the limit. The strain of living with a man who had become totally different than the one she had married was a heavy burden to bear. My self pity had consumed me. I had become my own worst nightmare. I was my own worst enemy. The "enemy" I now fought was "in-a-me."

As a soldier I had been trained to protect myself with shields. And now I had shielded my heart and my emotions. Nothing Ruth could do or say could penetrate the walls I built. Along with losing my arm I had lost my self respect. And, since I did not respect myself, I did not respect those around me.

My dreams had been displaced by despair. My hopes were distant memories. I believed that I was a failure. I had lost my arm. I had lost my faith, and Ruth had lost her husband.

Suddenly, out of nowhere , my twelve year old son, Amos, ran into my room. Amos was a twelve year old bundle of life! His coal black hair was flying in every direction. His dark eyes were flashing with excitement as he tried to catch his breath. I was reminded of how excited I was when he was born. I once had high hopes for Amos. But, when part of me died, it robbed him of the father he deserved.

He grabbed both sides of my face to get my attention. His mouth was moving but the words would not come! It seemed unusual that a boy who normally had a million things to say could not speak. He wanted me to pay attention to him so badly! He kept saying, "The soldiers are here, the soldiers are here!"

He desperately wanted to see me get excited about something, about anything! He missed our games. He missed our laughter. He missed his father!

My attitude had turned our home into a place of walking on pins and needles, and Amos was hoping that this news would lift my spirits. I tried my best to act happy but, this was not good news to me. Having to see soldiers again was like adding insult to injury. It would just open the old wounds.

As Amos, Ruth and I walked outside to greet our guest, we really were surprised to find out that this was not just any band of soldiers needing water. It was my old Commander, Benjamin, who had come to see me.

And then it happened. My great friend and leader spoke the words I'll never forget.

"Jason," he looked deep into my eyes, "How would you like to get back into the battle again?"

For a moment the earth stood still.

I was overcome with emotion. Great, mixed emotions. As we stood under the fig trees in the cool afternoon breeze my mind was awash with memories. Benjamin had always been like my big brother. We had grown up together in the foothills and had played "soldier" together for most of our childhood. It was a gift from God that he had become my commander in the unit I had chosen to serve in. More than once we had rescued one another. Our hearts had knit together long ago. He was always there for me! But that was then--and this was now.

For what seemed like an eternity, we just stared at each other, neither one knowing how the other would react. When we could bare it no longer, we embraced and we both laughed, to hold back the tears.

For a while it was like old times. What great adventures we replayed. What great battles and victories we relived! My blood actually felt like it was flowing again. My mind became alert. My pulse began to speed up as I remembered who and what I was!

He, of all people, knew my pain. He knew it might as well have been had my heart cut out rather than losing my arm.

He also knew that I'd let my life go totally downhill. I'd lost my dreams. I had no vision for the future.

My first and immediate thought was "No!"

My glory days were all behind me. Just faded memories. Echoes that were uncomfortable and unwelcome. Just a "ghost" from the past.

Benjamin startled me when he once again asked, "Jason, I'm serious. How would you like to get back into the battle again?"

I wondered, "Why would he tease me so?"

I could no longer contain it. I reeled with anger and asked, "How could you? You know I can never use a sword again! I'll never be what I once was! My arm!"

I waved my stump in his face. "I have no arm! There is no place for men like me. I can never fight again!"

He grabbed me by the shoulders. He shook me so hard I would have hit him if I had a hand!

Chapter Four
I Am A Soldier

"Listen," He said, "I've come to the realization that far too many great men are wasting their lives sitting under fig trees waiting to die! Jason, we leaders have made a great mistake!"

"You were not a great warrior because of your sword. **You were a great warrior because of what is in your heart. You still have the heart of a warrior. You still have the mind of a winner. A champion is not defined by his physique. A champion is defined by his spirit.** And, I know, Jason that way down inside of you--way down inside that secret place that you don't even want to visit anymore--you still want to make a difference with your life! Am I right?"

"What on earth can I do?" I yelled! "I refuse to clean the camp and listen to the stories of battle. I...am...a...soldier!"

Each of us held our breath. After a long pause, I realized what I had said. I **AM** a soldier. Not **WAS** a soldier. I **AM** a soldier! And, for the first time in several years, I smiled a genuine smile. For the first time in years I was not defining myself by my wounds.

My good friend and mentor saw my immediate transformation. I was standing up straight. My voice was stronger and clear. The pain of the past was suddenly being set to the side because someone cared enough about me to look me in the eye and tell me my life was not over. My wounds were real. My pain was real. But, so was my future!

"What do you have in mind?" I asked.

"I want to form an elite group of men. I will choose them all. They all must be good men, tried and true. They all, like you, must have been dealt a serious blow. They must all have lived through the pain of loss and career devastation. There are hundreds just like you who have lost the use of their right arm. They, like you will become "Lefthanded Soldiers!"

I smiled at the thought. An elite group indeed. An elite group of "wounded warriors" coming out of retirement, getting back into battle shape, and striking fear into the hearts of men everywhere! Ha!

"And what will we do?" I asked. Make ugly faces and wave our stumps in unison. I stuck out my tongue and waved my partial arm at him. He could not help but laugh with me.

He said ""Remember when we were kids. We spent hours every day playing with our slings. We threw so many rocks our arms got so tired we could hardly lift them."

"Yea, so..."

"What did we do then?"

"We'd set up targets and try to throw with our left hands." And suddenly it hit me. The sling! The national past time of our children. We could actually sling a stone for several hundred feet! Shepherds used them to ward off lions and bears.

My thoughts raced back to when we were small children. Benjamin and I would hunt together. Late one evening while were sleeping out under the stars a loud noise awakened us. A hungry lion had seen our fire and more importantly had smelled our food. We ran for a nearby tree, but I stumbled and fell. This old mangy lion immediately headed in my direction. I was in a panic!

Out of nowhere I heard a whistling sound and a rock came flying through the air. It flew right past my head and struck the lion right between the eyes. She fell three feet from me!

I looked at her carcass and then over at Benjamin. I laughed a nervous laugh and screamed in relief, "I'm alive!" A lifelong tradition was born! "I'm alive!"

Somehow it only seemed right that the same young man who saved my life way back then would show up at my doorstep, and literally save my life again. And, as in the past, the sling was the weapon of choice.

"Jason" he said, "a 'Lefthanded Soldier' who can sling a stone, is still a soldier. This is not a joke. It will take hundreds of hours of practice. It will take great will and courage. Some of your fellow soldiers will laugh at you. You'll be told to go back and sit under the fig tree again. But, I believe that you will now have insights that they don't have. You'll have understanding that they don't have. Because you have walked through things that they have not, you will be able to relate to men in the midst of battles in ways that some men will never know."

"Jason, if you are willing and you want to really "feel alive" again, then let's get busy and find more men like you.

I want seven hundred men--chosen men, lefthanded--who can learn to sling a stone at a hair's breath and not miss. The enemy will never know what hit them!"

Chapter Five
Bitter...or better?

After talking with Ruth and Amos, I came to the realization that the part of me that was missing was not as important as the part of me that was left. Without realizing it, I had let this one unfortunate event define the rest of my life.

I relived it daily. Why did it happen? What could I have done differently? Should I have trained harder? Why did God let this happen? Why didn't somebody help me after I was hurt? Maybe it would have saved my arm? My life had become a life filled with questions that had no answers. When I gazed into a looking glass my eyes were immediately drawn to my arm. Once … I had seen a strong proud man with broad shoulders and a firm square jaw. For several years now, in my own eyes, I had only seen a weak, one armed man. Ruth never saw me that way. To Amos, I was still a hero. But, my perception had become my reality. **I was taking inventory of my "needs" and not taking stock of my "seeds."** Life was about what I did not have and not what I still had. It was sad to know that I not only lost my arm that day. I had lost who and what I was. I had been so focused on "what had been", that I could not see "what could be."

In my confused mind I had no future to look forward to. No dreams. No ambitions. For several years now I had been only a ghost of what I once was. Yes, I was breathing, but I was not alive. I was "the living dead." The word "hopeless" is an interesting word. When you lose "hope" you become "less."

Things would be different now! I would change. Benjamin's words had pierced my heart , and opened it! I would no longer let my past define my future. I would not let the man who injured me determine my destiny. He won that battle, but he would not win the war! I would become better lefthanded then I ever was right handed.

I would change. I would train more than I ever had in the past. I would renew my mind. I would gather rocks. I would strengthen my arm. I would practice till I could sling a stone at a single hair and never miss. I was a chosen man. Now I had a chance to "be" more and "do" more than I ever had before. I was not a loser. I was a soldier--a Lefthanded Soldier!

Benjamin was right. I had a reason to live! From now on I would be grateful and I would appreciate every day. Never again when I saw a comrade who was wounded and hurting would I look away in disgust at his weakness. I would remember that **he would not have been wounded if he had not cared enough to fight.** And fighting meant exposing his arm, and his life to injury and wounding.

And finally it was time to commit. I looked Benjamin right square in the eyes. We both knew what was next! As I had done as a child after Benjamin saved me, I shook myself and screamed at the top of my lungs, "I'm alive!" Ruth dropped her plate of bread and olive oil. Amos ran out under the fig tree to see what was happening. Benjamin looked up at me and we both shouted it again. "I'm alive!" It was just a start, but it sure felt good.

I was not prepared for what happened next. Rumors of our band of seven hundred chosen lefthanded men began to spread. We were not necessarily met with great enthusiasm. People began to talk. Who do these men think they are? They are too old. They've been hurt. Don't they know when to quit?

Instead of being thrilled that we were turning our lives around, some laughed us to scorn. We became fodder for their stories. They could think of every reason why we had no business getting all "fired up" again.

We looked at it differently. When one of our swords was damaged in battle the smiths put it into a fire again and forged it and repaired it. We Lefthanded Soldiers would not "retire." We, like our weapons of old, would "refire!"

Many wondered out loud why we couldn't let well enough alone. Hadn't we learned our lesson? Why risk another injury. Don't these soldiers know they might get hurt again?

There were even times when well meaning friends and family, tried to talk us out of it. Each day we had to guard our minds and our hearts. I learned that "friendly fire" is just as dangerous as that which comes from the enemy.

As a unit we made a decision to absolutely refuse to let these onslaughts deter us. We would not let these contaminated catapults of fear and doubt keep us from our duties. If our lives were to change, we had to change. We had to be diligent. Focused. We would not let anyone, anywhere steal our dreams! It would not be fear or desperation that would determine our destiny. It would be our decision to change. From inside our hearts we unlocked the door to change. And from inside our hearts we could lock out the fears of others. So, when someone delivered doubt to our doorsteps we simply refused to accept the package!

The strangest thing of all was when we reported to the battle camp for duty. Even our fellow soldiers were leery of us.

They whispered "If they were so good why did they get wounded in the first place?"

Some said "Do we really want to be known as the kind of army who needs the help of 'these kind of people'?"

They wondered how we would react when the battle was raging. Would "the ghost of the past" spook us and drive us from the battlefield?

None the less we spent each day preparing. Soon the battle would begin.

Chapter Six
I'm Alive!

"I'm alive!" I screamed at the top of my lungs! "I'm alive!"

Sunrise was here, breakfast was ready and the day of battle was at hand!

I threw back the flaps of my tent and stepped outside. I grabbed my sling and began to swing it in a circular motion. Around and around it went. It made a high pitched singing noise as it spun its circle. Soon, I heard another. Then another. Before long, there were seven hundred slings whirling around and around announcing to the world that our band of Lefthanded Solders was "alive and well!" We were ready.

There was movement in every direction . Thousands of men and their armaments were making ready. We each gathered under our banners. Our 700 men gathered together. Each of us had different backgrounds. But we all had one thing in common. We had been wounded. And, each and every one of us, had determined to turn our lives around and become champions in battle once again.

I was filled with mixed emotions. Part of me wanted to laugh. Part of me wanted to cry.

I thought of Ruth and Amos. I thought about my home. I thought of how my suffering had caused them to suffer. Never again! I resolved to never again allow myself to become a "victim." From this day forth I would be a "victor."

Apart from battle, I would spend the rest of my life telling others that times of testing were common to us all. I would remind them that the greater the test, the greater the testimony! The greater the battle the greater the victory! I would tell them that no one, anywhere, anytime, had the right to make any one of us feel like we are less then we are.

I would tell the bruised, battered, and brokenhearted that they could change. If they would change the way they saw themselves it would change the way they saw others. It would change the way they saw life! I would tell them that I had chosen to wear a victor's crown and not a victim's curse. And they could make that choice also.

But a victor's crown is only worn by those who've been to war. And today was the day of battle.

Benjamin stood on a great rock in our midst. He raised his arms above his head and an immediate hush fell across the entire encampment.

His voice roared like the thunder! "Today...we fight!"

The roar of 10,000 men rang out in approval.

"Today, we all, great and small, from the east and from the west, from the north and from the south, we are all in one accord. Today, we are not many armies. Today, we are one army."

The standard bearers began to wave the banners as warriors from all across the land began to smite their hands against their breastplates in agreement.

Then Benjamin looked in our direction. A smile danced across his battle worn face. "Today, we welcome back the heroes of the past! For today, they will help us all determine our destiny!"

700 slings began to whirl around and around in unison!

A swell of emotion swept through the camp as this **"once" great army, again became "one" great army.**

The trumpets sounded. And we began our slow march into history.

Chapter Seven
A Lesson From History

*Among all this people there were seven hundred chosen men **lefthanded**; every one could sling stones at a hair breadth, and not miss.*

Judges 20:16

Yes, my friends, this story is historically accurate. It's chronicled in the ancient book of Judges. A small section of this book talks about an army. It was a very special army that represents many other unique armies just like them. It's a story of seven hundred men. Seven hundred "chosen" men. These writings say that each one of these men was lefthanded. And it says these seven hundred chosen lefthanded men could throw a stone at a hair breath and not miss.

When I first read this all too brief narrative, something did not make sense. That was a very unique story. I was intrigued! Why would an army recruit seven hundred lefthanded men? And, why would it teach them all the same vocation? I knew this culture revered the "right hand." Their writings declared that the honored men would sit on the "right" hand of the King. The sheep would be on the "right" hand and the "goats" on the left hand. There was more to this than my eyes were seeing. I began to read other translations and search the original language that this account had been written in.

Here is what I found. These particular men were from the tribe of Benjamin. A traditional thought is that all Benjamites were lefthanded. That's ludicrous. Tradition teaches that, but history does not teach that. The word "Benjamin" itself means "son of the right hand!"

So I read a Jerusalem translation of this story because sometimes we as Westerners don't see things from the Eastern view point. And the Jerusalem Bible said there were seven hundred chosen men who could throw lefthanded or right handed.

So I said to myself, "What is missing? One translation says they're lefthanded, and one of them says they could throw with the left or right. What is the full story?"

I believe they were both correct. After my research I determined that the text obviously meant that at one time they could use both the left or right hand. They could use both hands. But "now" they were all lefthanded men.

I discovered that the word "lefthanded" in this context, in the original language presents a combination of words signifying literally, a man whose right hand is impeded or lame, who therefore uses the *left hand instead.

I also discovered that Jean Leclerc, a noted encyclopedist observes, that "the 700 lefthanded men seem therefore to have been made slingers, because they could not use the right hand, which is employed in managing heavier arms; and they could discharge the stones from the sling in a direction against the opponents who were not on their guard, and thus do the greater execution."

Why is that important? Let's stop and think. We know that in ancient days all soldiers had helmets on. They all had breastplates on. Their loins were covered with leather girdles. They had shoes on, and they had leggings to guard their shins. They had the shield in their hands and either swords or spears. Predominately, the society was right handed. In fact, in those days being lefthanded was not a good thing! Remember, "the goats were on the left and the sheep were on the right." Being lefthanded was frowned upon!

---

*Another term for lefthanded as used in the Judges account is "Itter yad yemeeno." It too means obstructed in his right hand. So we now understand the Chaldee Targum, "gemid beedaih deyammeena," contracted or impeded in his right hand."

People didn't want to be lefthanded because it was looked down upon. The right hand got the blessings. There's a lot of misunderstanding about this.

What was happening? Stop and think. If you had your head covered, your chest covered, your waist covered, your legs covered, and you had a shield up, what was the most exposed part of a warrior when he went into the field? His right arm! So, if it was the most exposed area in battle, what was the most often wounded part? The right arm!

In those days, if you could not use a sword, or if you could not throw a spear, your battle worthiness was questioned. Many men got their right arm injured. Sometimes it was cut off. Many times the wound would severe the nerves, or damage a muscle. If he could not use that arm he was no longer an asset. Many times he retired from service. He would no longer be a soldier because he could not use the sword, or the spear. Proud warriors did not want to be relegated to menial tasks.

But somewhere along the line there was a wise leader like Benjamin. He thought, now wait a minute, it wasn't the right arm that made a warrior great. These men still have a warrior's mind. They still have a warrior's heart. And just because they can't do what they used to do because they've been wounded, is no reason to take these great warriors and set them on the shelf.

Benjamin believed that too many good men had basically gone into retirement. They only talked about the good old days. They were unhappy. He realized that the army needed them if it was to continue to win battles.

But, they were hurt. So, Benjamin decided that something was wrong with this picture. The army needed men of valor and strength. So, this great and wise leader brought all of those wounded warriors back into service. He taught them to use the other hand. And they got so good that they could sling a stone at a hair breath and not miss!

I want you to let your imagination go for a minute. See the enemy coming toward the battle ground. See all of the flags, and all of the banners waving! Listen now, and hear the sound of the horses' mighty hooves pounding the earth, and listen as the armaments of war are being prepared. Hear all of the trumpets!

The enemy is coming over the ridge and gets his first glimpse of your army, and the first thing they see is a bunch of little one armed, lefthanded guys swirling their slings. I want you to see them laughing. Hear them ask, "Where are the real soldiers?"
But in the distance I want you to hear the whirl of seven hundred slings going round and round! Swish, swish, swish.

The enemy says , "Today we'll feed you to the fowls of the air"

Swish, swish, swish.
As they get closer they yell ."Today we'll make you food for the worms of the earth!"

Swish, swish, swish.

And BAM! BAM! BAM!

Seven hundred stones come flying out, and seven hundred enemy soldiers fall over. Now it was a whole different story. Who's laughing now?

Benjamin taught these "wounded warriors" to decide to use the best of what they had. He taught them to put the wounds of the past behind them, and draw the line in the sand. Enough self pity, enough "if only's." What's done is done.

This great leader convinced them to get back into the "fray" again. Live like a warrior again! Be a winner again! He taught them to bury the ghost of the past.
He reminded them that they still had a warrior's mind, and a warrior's heart.

They became heroes! They went from zero to hero because a leader cared enough to look past their wounds, to look past their disappointments, to look past their failures, and see inside of them. Inside, there was still the heart of a winner.

Today, there are "wounded warriors" still among us. I would like to think that there are still leaders who are wise enough to know that these "wounded" can become Lefthanded Soldiers. They already have a wealth of experience. They are winners that just need somebody to love them enough and care enough to once again help them engage in life. They just need leaders.

Chapter Eight
I'm A Lefthanded Soldier

"Knock, knock."

"Who's there?"

"Tick."

"Tick who?'

"Tick 'em up, I'm a tongue-tied towboy!"

As a young boy that was my favorite "knock, knock" joke.
I liked it because it fit me to a tee. Or, maybe it was
because it did not fit me that I liked it. You see, one of my
earliest memories is the doctor whispering to my mom.
"He needs his tongue clipped."

"What do you mean?" She asked.

He opened my mouth and said that my tongue was tied all
the way to the front. Not all the way across, but, none the
less, it was tied down and I would not be able to speak
clearly. He asked her if I had tried to talk yet.

She just laughed. She said, "Doctor, the problem is not getting him to talk--it's getting him to shut up!"

So, the Doctor and I had a great conversation. He kept shaking his head. This is not right. This kid is not supposed to be talking this well. So, it became a family joke. I would tell my "knock, knock" joke and stick my tongue out. Except I could not stick my tongue out. It was tied down.

And to this day, I still cannot stick out my tongue. It's probably for the best. I've been able to get into enough trouble as it is. And, I do understand trouble.

You see, I am a Lefthanded Soldier. Like many of you, in some areas of my life, I have been wounded. At times these wounds have caused me to fail miserably. More than once I've been wounded. More than once. I know what it's like to "fight the good fight," yet get beat up, bruised, and battered. I know what it feels like to give it my best shot but lose, and be hurt so deeply I did not want to live. I know what it's like to **want** to quit. I know what it's like to be **forced** to quit. But, by the grace of God, I know what it's like to turn my life around and become a champion once again. Yes, I am a Lefthanded Soldier. And, like Benjamin, I'm looking for others to join me.

A lefthanded soldier is anyone who has been wounded in life...whether physically, emotionally, spiritually, or
44

financially and yet, against all odds, has risen from the
devastation to become a champion!

I'm willing to tell my story, so you can see how utter
failure can lead to total success.

I was raised in Government funded projects. They were
stone cold, ugly, red brick buildings located in East Dallas.
My dad was a one hundred percent disabled Army veteran
whose monthly subsidy check was supplemented by my
mother's meager waitress check and tips. I don't mean this
disrespectfully, but I never saw my dad work a day in his
life. So, that planted a seed inside of me and it would later
bear much fruit. To say that we were poverty stricken was
an understatement. Government commodity meat was a
staple in our diet. Otherwise, we lived on "icebox stew."
That's where you open the icebox and mix up whatever
was left and make it into a stew.

My dad's disability was a back injury. He had died several
times on the operating table and each time he was revived. I
slept many a night on the cold hard floor of the VA hospital
not knowing whether I would still have a dad the next day.

Because of the constant pain he endured, his best friend
became "Jack Daniel." He "spoke" with Jack the first thing
every morning. Just a little nip to get the 'ole engine
started he would laugh and say. I remember wondering

what was in that brown paper sack he carried around. Although my dad had a quick wit and a great and handsome smile, I quickly learned to hate alcohol because of the devastating toll it took on him and the rest of our family. Liver problems ran their course and his belly swelled to three times its normal size. He began to have terrible vomiting fits and throw up great quantities of blood and small portions of his insides. More than once I found him passed out in a pool of his own blood.

My mother worked as a waitress as long as I can remember. Milk at school was three cents a carton and it was Mama's tips that paid for it. Forty-five years ago a ten cent tip was important because it paid for milk for three of her four boys. Almost every night she worked until 9:00 pm. So we rarely saw her except on weekends. She had to clean and wash clothes all day Saturday and sleep all day Sunday! So the concept of "family" as we all know it was not part of my life. I basically raised myself. I never remember my Dad telling my mom that he loved her. I never heard my Mom tell my Dad she loved him.

I believe with all my heart that my Dad and Mom loved us kids. But, somewhere between "Jack Daniel", his pain and her exhaustion, love and affection were long gone. We lived in abject poverty and our only goal in life was survival. Just make it through the day.

Not only was I born into poverty, but unfortunately, poverty was born in me. It was all I had ever seen. It was all I ever expected. That spirit of poverty took root in me and convinced me to never, ever think big.

Between my Dad, my Mom and my brothers there were 13 marriages. Long lasting relationships were not something my family excelled at. It never paid off to get too involved in someone's life. It was only a matter of time before they would not be around. Broken dreams, broken promises, broken marriages, broken lives; and like Humpty Dumpty, it didn't seem anything or anybody could put it all back together again. So I was an unwilling participant in a life of brokenness. And just as poverty was planted inside of me and ultimately bore its ugly fruit, so were the seeds of brokenness buried in my heart. It was only a matter of time before the disappointments, failures and broken marriages that were the pillars of my past would inevitably become part of my future.

During high school I was an athlete, Chaplain of the Student Council, President of the Christian Athletes and, although nobody knew it I was fighting for my life. My mom had very suddenly been diagnosed with cancer and died soon after. My dad tried to hold things together but because he could not understand me always wanting to go to church, he and I were trying to live in two different worlds. You've heard of families having a "black sheep" in them? Well, I was the "white sheep" of the family. All I ever wanted was to do right. I refused to drink alcohol. I refused to smoke or engage in coarse conversation. I really wanted to please both God and man. I had a great zeal, but absolutely no knowledge of how to do that.

I moved in with a friend of mine whose dad was a pastor. I slept on the floor of the Sunday School room, when I slept at all. I worked from 11:00 pm till 8:00 am at the loading docks of Frito Lay. I drove to school in an old '59 Chevy that continued to run several minutes after you turned off the key. I attended school all day, practiced football, did my homework, slept for several hours and started all over again. Nobody at school knew I was doing this and over a period of time I fell from the pinnacle of success as an athlete and an honor student to becoming a divorced high school drop out joining the Marine Corps, so I could volunteer for Viet Nam. I just wanted to die! I figured that dying in battle, in the service of my country, would at least give my life some sort of meaning and dignity.

So, on April 1st, I reported for duty in the United States Marine Corps. Was I ever an April Fool!

No matter how I tried, I kept getting stationed in California! Dying in Camp Pendleton was not exactly the glorious exit I was preparing for! God does take care of fools.

Nothing is as empty as being broke--and broken--at the same time!

Chapter Nine
Change Is A Door

For most of my life, when I was wounded, I had waited for the right person or the right people to come along and help change my situation. The right person, the right time, the right circumstance, the right "something." I'm not exactly sure why. But, I've learned a marvelous lesson. ***Change is a door that can only be opened from the inside.*** No external force had the power to change me. No person. No circumstance. No "anything." All of these external forces could "offer" change, but change itself was to come from the inside. I was the only one who could unlock that door!

In the last one hundred twenty-five years, we've gone from the teepee of the American Indian to the Empire State Building. We've gone from Kitty Hawk to Mars! We've gone from sending smoke signals to the World Wide Web and bouncing video off satellites! Talk about change! We can send a message 24,000 miles around the world in a matter of seconds but sometimes it takes years for the same message to penetrate that last quarter inch of our sculls! It took years for this simple truth to set in: I must personally take responsibility to open my life to change and I must begin to pursue it with a whole heart!

I have learned that the size of your "mess" determines the size of your "message." The greater the adversity, the greater the victory! You cannot run before you walk. You cannot sing before you talk. Life demands that growth comes about through a process. Change is a process. So, I began the process. I chose to leave the world of poverty and brokenness behind.

It is a well known fact that to begin a journey you have to have directions. To decide on a direction you have to know exactly where you are starting from. I knew for sure what lay behind me. Where I had been was not the issue. So I took inventory of where I was and what I had. In other words I inventoried my "seeds" not my "needs." I had no formal education, but I was a great talker. So, after seeking counsel from several people (something new to me) I decided that my greatest attribute was talking. So, I decided to find a job talking. I thought about becoming a DJ. But I was told that I sounded like a cross between Elmer Fudd and Tim Conway. So, that was out. On the bright side I was also told that I had the perfect face for radio!

It was suggested that sales might be good for me. I could "sell" people on most anything I believed in. I remember when I got my first sales job selling storm windows.

Nobody told me it was supposed to be hard, so it wasn't! I did great. I was making about $800 a week, far more than I'd ever made before. I found out that I could sell a farmer an electric milking machine and take his only cow as a trade in! I got a taste of the free enterprise system and I began to dream big.

I happened to see an ad in a local paper that read, "Sales, $5,000 a week". That blew me away! I called and the lady asked me about my background and qualifications, then she politely screened me out.

"Sir, I'm sorry, but you don't qualify."

I couldn't believe it! I called right back and said, "You don't understand. I want an interview!"

She said, "You don't understand, you are not qualified." She hung up.

I called back and said, "You're making a horrible decision. You may be costing your company millions of dollars." I was on a roll. "You make $8 and hour and you're making a million dollar mistake." She hung up!

I called back! I said "Well, maybe you make $10 an hour!" She hung up. I was revved up by now! I would not be denied! I got a crisscross directory and looked up the address that had that phone number. I went to the office, looked that lady right square in the eye, told her my name, smiled real big, and told her that I was there for my interview!

She was flabbergasted! She said, "I told you that you are not qualified!"

I told her, "Do you see that chair over there? I'm going go sit down. And, sometime today, somebody will not show up for an interview. When that happens, I'll fill their slot!" All day long, I sat there.

The hiring manager kept walking out to meet with prospects and each time he would just stare at me. Finally, late that afternoon, he leaned across this lady's desk and whispered, "Who is that man?" She told him the entire story and he just smiled and shook his head. He walked over to me and stuck out his hand and said. "You're hired!" Anybody with that kind of bulldog tenacity, anybody that wants it that much, deserves a chance!"

I've heard it said that there has never, ever been a device created that could measure the size of a man or woman's heart. You just have to get it out of your heart and put it into action!

And because I chose to use this simple gift I have, other opportunities are constantly put before me! I'm reminded of what Douglas Fairbanks Jr. said. He once began a speech with one of the all time best opening lines: "I feel like a mosquito in a nudist colony. I look around and I know it's wonderful to be here, but I don't know where to begin." If you will use what you have, others gifts will spring up and great opportunities are in your future.

I learned that **if your vocation is not a vacation, you are destined to meander in mediocrity.** You have to love what you are doing.

So, I began to pursue only what I loved. I knew that I loved video, so, I produced a video to help market a product I was selling. I absolutely made the men I hired to do the actual taping and editing, etc. to explain every step of the video process to me. Amazingly, people began to call me from everywhere! They did not want my product but they loved my video! They began to ask me if I could produce one for them. So I said "Sure" and I "backed" into a love of mine-- the video business. Now, I own my own production company, all of my own equipment and have made untold videos for major companies all across America! Passionate pursuit produces results!

It worked so well with the videos, I set my belief in action again. I loved music. So I pursued song writing. At first, nobody gave me the time of day. But, I had learned that the greatest adversities preceded the greatest victories.

Let's look at some of the lyrics to a song that I wrote. It was born in the midst of these challenges.

The victor's crown only goes to those who've been in war.
Eagles can't stay in their nest if they want to soar.
Sitting on the side lines you'll never be your best.
You can't have a testimony 'till you've had a test.

God won't send thirst people to an empty well.
Heavens cup sure is sweeter once you've tasted hell.
There's no wine until the grape has gone
through the press.
You can't have a testimony 'till you've had a test.
                                                    -- Gary Eby

I've learned the size of your mess really does determine the size of your message. It may not be pleasant to hear, but, the size of your testimony is due, in large part, to the size of your test. Where would Abe Lincoln have been without the Civil War? Where would John Kennedy have been without the Cuban Missile Crises? David needed Goliath to become King. You cannot not wear a victor's crown without having fought a few battles!

Eventually, not only this song, but many others were recorded. They've been sung on television, radio, and concert stages all over the world. I believe now that God wants us to succeed in everything we do!

I began to pursue another passion. I wanted to use the "mess" I made of my life as a means to present a message. So I began to speak at business meetings, network marketing meetings, seminars, churches, conventions and anywhere the doors would open. I believe that the proof of you being passionate about something is that you actually begin to pursue it! Now, I've spoken all across America, in Brazil, Japan and England. And I'm just getting started! Not bad for a "tongue tied towboy, huh?

I now have a beautiful wife of over 24 years and a family that is blessed beyond measure. My video company has produced numerous network marketing tools, my music publishing company has blossomed with numerous songs being recorded, and my speaking company all provide us a blessed and prosperous life by allowing me to encourage and build up people's lives.

Why do I tell you this? Because I've learned that just because I was a wounded, broken man, sitting on the sidelines of life did not mean I had to stay there. I would learn other things! I would train hard! I would improve! I would change. I would be a Lefthanded Soldier!

Now, I am the leader that finds and recruits others. And together we will build an army that will change the world!

Chapter Ten
Finish The Race

From time to time I encounter others (fellow soldiers) that will not allow me to put my past behind me.

Their judgmentalism and anger over events and situations that are over thirty years old is unfortunate. I wish I could tell you that it never bothers me. That would be a lie. There are times when I'm physically exhausted, or I'm dealing with the challenge of trying to make a difference in someone's life, that someone blind sides me with a "ghost of the past." I've learned that when I feel like quitting to take a deep breath and remember a great lesson I learned as a young man.

As a young man I loved sports. My passion was football. But, I also played baseball, basketball, and ran track. I was fast. In fact, **the older I got, the better I was!** And, because my dad was a disabled veteran, he sometimes participated "vicariously" through my exploits.

I remember this one particular season that I won race after race. I ran the 440 yard dash, which is commonly called "the race for insane people." Why? Because if you try to sprint the entire race, you might have a "myocardial infarction". And, if you try to pace yourself, you would lose! So what do you do? You tear out of the starting blocks and hope that you survive!

Race after race I would win. My Dad would sit up in the bleachers and cheer. He could hardly walk up and down the stairs, but he would sit and watch me, and in his heart, it was him running down there.

This particular meet was the city championship. Everybody was there and I had on my blue silk shorts, my little blue silk top, and my track cleats. I had drawn the inside lane. A lane is an area set apart for people to run in. Each person is in a different lane. In the 440 they do what they call staggering the lanes, because the runners in the outside lanes would have to run farther if they did not stagger the lanes.

It wouldn't be fair if they lined up straight across because the runners on the outside would have further to run. So, the runner in each lane gets to start a little ahead of the one inside of him.

The guy in the first lane started at exactly 440 yards. The next guy got 4 or 5 yards in front, and so on. Everyone is staggered out, so they would all run equal distance.

I was in the inside lane and boy, I was ready. This was it. My dad was up in the bleachers watching. My heart felt like it was beating out of my chest. I know his heart was pounding, also.

"That's my boy, that's my boy, that's my boy." He just knew I was going to win.

And suddenly, it was time to run!

"On your mark, get set..."

I looked down my lane and I could see all of the runners in the other lanes because they were all staggered on the outside of me.

BAM! The gun went off and I tore out as fast as I could. Immediately, because others were going to pace themselves, I was already making up the stagger! And then, the unthinkable happened.

The trainer of one of the athletes out in the far lane ran out on the track to get his starting blocks. I came out of the blocks so fast I ran right into that trainer. There was no way that I should have gotten there that fast. He should never have been there. But I was, and he was. To say we both fell is an understatement. We rolled for what seemed like fifteen minutes! It was like I was in a slow motion vacuum! It was ethereal!

Of course, everybody else kept running! People ran over me and cleated me with their spikes in the back of my legs and the back of my head. I had huge cinder burns on my elbows and knees from the track and I was bleeding in numerous places! And all of this happened in a flash.

The world was spinning! The crowd was gasping. What was I going do?

As my eyes slowly began to focus, I looked up and I saw my dad. His eyes were as big as silver dollars. I was gathering my thoughts. And suddenly, I did all I knew how to do. Every instinct inside of me said to get up and run. I looked up and I was 20 yards behind. That's like a mile in a race like this! My hair stood up on my arms. I gritted my teeth. Tears were coursing down my face. I was hurting-- physically, mentally and emotionally.

I ran and I ran. I ran like the wind. I felt like "Jim Thorpe, All American" a movie I had seen on television. I passed a guy. And I passed another guy...and then another! We got to the backstretch and I passed another guy and yet another!

The crowd was going wild! We came around the far curve. This is where you hit the proverbial "wall!" This is where your lungs are in rebellion and your heart is screaming! Your legs are saying, "Mercy"! Have mercy on us!"

I blocked out all the pain and kept on running...and I kept passing people. This was Hollywood at its best.

I was ten yards from the finish line and could barely focus my eyes to see it.

Keep running Gary. Don't quit. Push through the tape. You can do this. Only five more yards. Three more!

It was amazing. What a finish! Three of us crossed the finish line, all within one yard of each other. I was spent. I had given my all. But, I came in third place.
The crowd was going crazy, but my heart was broken. I was cramping. I could not get my breath. Was this a dream? This could not be happening. Not to me! But, it was real. I had lost.

My despair was overwhelming. I felt empty. I felt totally alone. I hurt in places I did not know I had! I wanted to cry. I felt like I had done everything wrong. I couldn't bear to turn and look up into the stands at my dad. I couldn't look him in the eye. In my eyes, I had failed.

I just remember going over to the infield and taking my sweats and pulling them over my head and just curling up into the fetal position. I remember feeling like I wanted to die. My skin had huge cinder burns on my elbows from the fall. My knees were bleeding. I had holes and perforations in my legs from the other runners. I had holes in the back of my head. My lungs were hurting. Every cell in my body was crying out "why did you do that to me?"

I peeked out of my sweat shirt and I saw my dad coming down the stairs. What a sight. He had little bitty spindly legs . His belly was swollen from cirrhosis of the liver to four times its normal size. His back had been broken and he'd died on the operating table three times. Here he was climbing down the steps, climbing over a fence, and walking across the track to me. And I broke. Like a fountain of pent up emotions, I broke. I couldn't stand it. What would I say? What would I do? I lost. I knew he would be so disappointed!

He slowly but surely knelt down beside me and put his arms around me. I cried for the first time in my life on my father's shoulder. I kept saying "Daddy, I'm so sorry. Oh, I'm so sorry. I'm so sorry. I'm sorry, I fell."

I tried to explain and it just wouldn't come out. He just listened and let me finish. Finally, I pulled the sweats down and I looked him in the eye and said, "Dad, I'm sorry, Daddy, I fell. I lost."

He looked at me and said some words that I'll never forget. Words that I've taught my children to say, and I want to teach you to say. He said, "Gary, you finished the race! You were hurt, and you didn't quit. You fell, and you didn't quit. You were bleeding, and you didn't quit. You had spike marks on your legs, and you didn't quit. You had scars in your head, and you didn't quit. Your heart was broken, and you didn't quit. You were disappointed, and you didn't quit. When every reason in the world said, **'Quit,'** you got up and finished the race."

He said, "Today, in my eyes you are more a winner than any race you've ever won."

That day I learned that when life knocks you to your knees, you get up again and finish the race.

That has been a lesson that has stuck with me all of my life. I can't tell you how many times in business, and as a songwriter, in my marriage and as a father, I have faced adversity. I cannot tell you how many times I have failed. Sometimes it was my fault. Sometimes it wasn't. Sometimes I just made a stupid decision. Sometimes it was because I refused to accept counsel. Sometimes it was because I was a bullheaded ex-Marine. But for whatever reason, I failed.

Time after time after time, in my moments of desperation, in my moments of wanting to quit, in my moments of saying, "I'll never ever, ever do this again," I can still hear my dad say, "Finish the race."

Chapter Eleven
Oh, Rats!

For most people it seems easier to just live in the "status Quo." The risks and uncertainties that change will bring will keep many from ever trying. They crashed once. From now on let's just keep the proverbial plane in the hanger. But planes were meant to fly. And you are the captain of your ship.

There was once a man who loved to fly. He decided to take a different kind of vacation one year. This time he decided he was going to drive. But a lifelong pilot, who is used to seeing things from the air, just got tired of the view from behind the steering wheel. After he had driven 10-15 hours, three or four days in a row, he couldn't stand it anymore.

He screamed to himself, "I've got to fly!"

Before long, on a long stretch of highway in the middle of nowhere, he drove past an airfield where he could rent an airplane.

He said, "This is it! I'm on vacation. I want to do something I enjoy."

So, he pulled the car over and rented an airplane. They began to check him out on the plane, but he was so excited about flying, he hardly paid attention. He got inside the plane and said, "Yeah, yeah, yeah, blah, blah, blah! I am a pilot, you know."

Once inside, he started the engine, took off as fast as he could and started flying around. It was wonderful...for a while. Things were going good, and then suddenly, he heard some squeaks.

He thought, "I don't particularly like that, but everything seems to be working fine.'' So he flew on, and again, after a while, he began to hear, "squeak, squeak, squeak." Now, I don't know about you, but that would make me a little bit nervous. You see, I don't really like to fly anyhow. The Bible says, "*Lo* I am with you always.'' I take that very seriously so I stay **low** to the ground! As this man kept flying, he kept hearing squeak, squeak, squeak.

And finally, he said to himself, "Something is wrong here." He looked again at his instrument panel. You have to have faith in your instrument panel. And one of the instruments failed.

"This is bad," he said. And it wasn't a few more minutes before another one failed and then, another one failed! He got on the radio, and he called the tower and said, "I've got all kinds of problems! My instruments are failing! I've got to land!"

And they said, "Relax. Tell us what happened."

He said, "I've been hearing all kinds of squeaking, squeaking, squeaking, and it's driving me crazy!"

Then they said, "What instruments are failing?"

He said, "This one failed then this one failed, then another one failed!"

The tower replied emphatically, "Listen to us! Don't argue with us! You pull back, and you climb as high as you can!"

He said, "You don't understand! All I want to do is get back down to the ground. And you're telling me to go higher?"

And they said, "We want you to go higher. Higher than you've ever been before. You pull back and climb!"

And he began to argue with them. And they said, "You've been trained not to argue with us. Trust us. Now pull back!"

And although he knew that everything within his flesh wanted to land, inside his heart he knew to listen. He pulled back on the stick, and he climbed, and climbed, and climbed. And they said," Are you getting cold?"

He answered, "Yes, I'm getting cold!"

So they responded "Pull up higher. Go up higher!"

Then his wings started to freeze over, and he was freezing, and his teeth were chattering. And he thought, "If I don't die because of these stupid instruments, there's enough ice on the wings to cause me to crash!"

And finally they said, "Give us three more minutes!"

And as he was counting down he shouted , "I'm about to freeze! The wings are frozen! There's ice all over them!"

And they asked him, "Has the squeaking stopped?"

He says, "Yeah, I haven't even thought about it. I was so cold! The squeaking has stopped!"

And they said," OK, you can begin to lower the plane now." So he began to lower it bit by bit, and the ice began to melt.

He answered, "Yeah."

"Anymore instruments going out?"

"Absolutely not.'' he answered.

And finally he came to himself and asked, "What just happened?"

They said, "In this area, this time of year, we have a tremendous rat infestation. What had happened was some rats had crawled up inside the engine part of your airplane. And that squeaking you were hearing was those rats!

There were freaking out when your plane was climbing. All that wind was hitting them and they were freaking and squeaking!

That's what you were hearing. Then the rats began to look around and see all these wonderful wires and they decided to have lunch! They started chewing through your wires. And, based on what you were saying, we knew which wires they were chewing on, because of the instruments that were going out. First this one went out, then they chewed the next one and that one went out. We knew that if you tried to land they would have chewed through the next wires. So, before you could have ever landed you would have crashed. The only hope you had was climbing.

So the pilot asked, "Why is that?"

"Because you froze those suckers to death! By refusing to land, refusing to give in to your fear, you won! What was trying to kill you, was killed off instead!"

Now, isn't that the way it is with our life? We get into adversity, we think we've got everything under control, and then "BOOM," everything starts going wrong. Things start failing. And the first thing we want to do when we confront failure or a challenge, when we hit adversity, the first thing we want to do is "land the plane!"

"Let's go back to the way it was! It was easier when I wasn't a dreamer. It was easier when I didn't have these big visions. It was easier when I didn't have these goals!"

Let me tell you something. Any time you try to grow a muscle, you've got to break down that existing muscle first. Why do we do that? Because we know it will grow back stronger! Life has it's adversities. They can break us or, they can build us! We can get bitter...or better! We can break, or we can break through!

When a baby chick is born, it has to break free from the shell that's had it captive. If you intervene, and you take the shell off of the chicken without it struggling to get free, and you don't let him stretch his muscles by breaking out of the egg, the chicken will die. That struggle is part of his birthing process to build his strength. If you do it for the chicken and not let it "stretch," it'll die.

Sometimes we want people to take us through all of our problems. We don't want to deal with them. But, that's how you, like the chicken, die. Your "heart" is made stronger when you encounter adversity and fight until you prevail!

You have to take one step at a time. You have to stretch yourself to grow. And when everything starts failing, human nature tells you that the first thing you want to do is just go back to the way it used to be.

But the world is looking for leaders. Instead of landing the plane, just pull back on the stick! Make the decision to fly higher and go farther than you ever have before! Do more than you've ever done before. Don't stop what you're doing. Do more! Do more than you've ever done before. And absolutely, positively refuse to even consider quitting. Don't land the plane! **CLIMB! Don't let some rats destroy your love for flying high! CLIMB!**

Chapter Twelve
One More Push

You are closer than you think! Just pick up a sling and head for the battlefield!

I remember when my wife was giving birth to our second daughter. The first time we had a daughter, we went to a hospital. The second time we decided to use a midwife. Daddy was going be in there. Daddy was going to help her all the way through it. We breathed together. We worked together. We practiced. We went to Lamaz classes. I was going to cut the umbilical cord. I was going to be there!

Does anybody besides me ever have trouble hearing the word **"push"** without remembering that process? **Push, push, push, push, push!** It's amazing what a mother goes through. I could not give birth. And it's not because I'm not anatomically correct! I just don't think I could deal with it. What my wife went through was amazing!

Hour after hour. Push, after push. Sssssss, after Sssssss. (You Lamaz people know what I'm talking about)

Breathing...resting...pushing...praying...and more breathing... resting...pushing...praying !

I remember when it came to the place where it was almost time. The baby was so close. All my wife cared about was , "I just want this baby out!" Then the baby would "crown", and you could actually see it's head. And finally the midwife said, "One more push!"

And after that last final push, **what a relief!** My wife was so excited. I was excited! And I cut the umbilical cord. It was awesome!

And I said, "Darling, what can I do for you?"

And she says, "Go get me a cheeseburger and a vanilla milk shake!" How do you spell relief? C.H.E.E.S.E.B.U.R.G.E.R!

Here's my point. It's that one last push that gives birth. Too many times when a miracle is conceived inside of us, or we get a dream conceived inside of us, the adverse circumstances of life will try to abort those miracles and dreams. Other people who have failed seem to surround us. They have a real problem with us suddenly being so success motivated. It's easier for them to bring you down than it is for them to "rise up" and be somebody!

Some people get right to the edge of the birth process for their dream. They are "one push away" from a miracle! It's just about time. They've paid the price. They've laid the foundation. They've helped a lot of people. It's almost time for their life, their dream, and their finances to explode, **and they quit!** What a tragedy! One push away!

Some of you are either at that place, or have been there. It's time to turn it around. You've gone through the adversity. You've grown. Your "baby" has gotten big inside of you. It's gotten so big that you can't keep it inside anymore. And just one more push and you're going have an awesome breakthrough financially, and in every area of your life. Please don't quit.

And for all of those of you who are sitting on the shelf of life. You're disengaged. Those of you who have been wounded. Those of you who have had your heart broken. Get up! Shake yourself! Get back into the battle of life one more time. And make that one last push. It'll not only change your life, it'll change your kids' lives, and your grandkids' lives. And that's way too big to let somebody else cause your dream to die.

Chapter Thirteen
Wounded Warriors

Let me speak personally to all those that know you're a wounded warrior. Maybe you've had your heart broken.

Sometimes it was someone else's fault, sometimes it was your fault. All I want to tell you is that you can still be a Lefthanded Soldier. It may not be like it once was for whatever reason. But, you can get back into the battle again! You can still have a dream in your heart.

You still have a warrior's heart! You still have a warrior's mentality. You still want life to be better for you. Don't you? You still want life to be better for your kids? Don't you want to make a difference in your life and in the lives of people who come into your path? Don't you want to make a difference? You can't do it sitting on the shelf. Let me be like a "Benjamin" to you. So, I have to say, and I want to say it in love, "Get over it! Put it behind you!" Draw the line in the sand and get back into the action again. If you have to take a baby step, do that! But, do something that puts you back into the battle again.

It will make a difference in your life, and in others. And when you make a difference in other people's lives, the law of the harvest will create a positive cycle that will come back into your life many times over.

One of the greatest Presidents in our nation's history, Abraham Lincoln, experienced failure, after failure in his life, but yet, he kept coming back, and history remembers him ending up as a winner. Because Lincoln chose to put his failures and wounding behind him, he became a Lefthanded Soldier. Our country withstood one of it's greatest trials because of his leadership. The proverbial loser had become the ultimate winner, and helped change the world. And you can, too.

Everything you've always wanted is right in front of you. Become a lefthanded soldier and before you know it, you'll be at the front of the army, the hero that will take the lead in the next battle!

Special Message from the Author

There are few things in life that move me like seeing someone overcome adversity. It reaches a part of me that nothing else can. When I finally realized that it gave me a clue to my life assignment. Without sounding arrogant, I believe that I've been called, gifted and equipped to reach out to anyone who has been wounded and bring them a message of renewal.

I believe that there are great men and women from all walks of life, who, because of some "event" or series of events, have pretty much given up. They have allowed their circumstances to condemn them to a life of "what-ifs." Somewhere between brokenness and bitterness they have laid down their proverbial swords and surrendered.

I just cannot sit idly by and let that happen!

How many great leaders are no longer leading? What will our society suffer because the leadership we need is somewhere hurting rather than rallying the troops?

What great sickness is raging because the doctors and nurses who can make a difference are needing healing themselves?

How many great sermons will not be preached because an overworked and underpaid Pastor had a "humpty-dumpty" fall and is allowing condemnation to keep him out of service?

Great public servants, teachers, volunteers, entrepreneurs, and politicians, all over the world are waiting...waiting for someone to care enough to put their arms around them and say, "Let's get back into the battle of life again! We need you!"

How do I know this? Because I've been there! I've failed in every area of life that is possible! But, by the grace of God, I've been able to rise from my ashes of despair to a level of success I never dreamed possible.

Because of that I can't help but want every hurting, disappointed man or woman I meet to look "past their past" and look toward the future full of faith.

Out of this compulsion "Lefthanded Soldiers " was born. I want to teach you to teach others that "Change is a door that can only be opened from the inside!"

Let's build an army of renewed, revived warriors. Let's teach them that they can make a decision to "engage" in life again. Let's teach them that they can make a difference in the world. They can be "Lefthanded Soldiers!"

Bonus Chapters

Your background doesn't matter. Your age, sex, economic status, or any other reason you can think of doesn't matter. Because you are a part of the human race you are subject to the challenges of life. We all have encountered Lefthanded Soldiers. Many of us have joined the ranks.

Because of that, I've chosen to add some Bonus Chapters, that while they are specific to certain vocations, I believe that each will resonate with all of us. So, while you may not be involved in these professions, the lessons will surely still be applicable to your lives.

Bonus Chapter One
For Educators and Trainers

It's been said that there are no bad students…only bad teachers.

In a world where learning is revered it seems an oxymoron that sometimes teachers are not. Many educators and even corporate trainers are not only expected to teach others, but continually educate themselves! It can be overwhelming. Many, like Jason, are retiring to "the fig tree." Many are defaulting to mediocrity. Many have grown wary of unappreciative students and clients. But in reality, we are still being taught. Somebody is always teaching. We are always learning.

But, if the "gifted" and "truly called" teachers have grown weary and wounded, exactly what are we learning, and from who? Are we content to let the media Madonna, or Madison Avenue mold our minds? No! We need real teachers!

I heard a story once about a major university that conducted an experiment. They took a select group of students and required them to wear some custom fitted glasses for a predefined time. The unusual thing about these glasses is that it made everything the students saw appear to them upside down. Of course, at first they were totally disoriented. Their food was upside down so they could not eat without help. Their books were upside down so they could not read. They had to have help getting to and from class and going to the restroom was a comedy of errors.

After about a week to ten days, at least they were able to gain their equilibrium. The nausea left and they could function to a certain degree on their own. So they were approached by the faculty and asked to continue the test for another month. They were being paid, so they agreed. After another month an amazing thing happened. The students could now read upside down. They could write upside down and were now able to attend classes on their own. This gives great credibility to the power and adaptability of the human mind. They lived in an upside down world, so their mindset was to learn to function in an upside down world. They responded in kind by thinking upside down.

So, if people can be made to think, imagine, and believe upside down, how difficult is it to believe that we can be programmed or develop a mindset to do things in a straight forward, successful manner? It's all in what you pour into your mind and let get settled. For that, we need our teachers back in the trenches leading us into battle!

Gifted…called…and HEALED, teachers. Renewed. Revived! Pursuing excellence!

I heard about a story that happened years ago. There was an elementary school teacher named Mrs. Thompson. On the very first day of school, in her 5th grade class she told the children a lie. Just like most teachers, she looked at all of her students and told them that she loved them all the same.

In the front row, slumped in his seat, was a little boy named Teddy Stoddard. She had watched Teddy the year before and noticed that he didn't play well with the other children, that his clothes were messy and that he constantly needed a bath. And boy, could Teddy be unpleasant. It got to the point where Mrs. Thompson would actually enjoy marking his papers with a broad red pen, making huge, bold X's and then putting a big "F" at the top of his papers. She would teach him a thing or two.

At the school where Mrs. Thompson taught, she was required to review each child's past records and she put Teddy's off until the very last. But, when she did review his file, she was in for a surprise. Teddy's first grade teacher wrote, "Teddy is a bright child with a ready laugh. He does his work neatly and has good manners. He is a joy to be around." His second grade teacher wrote, "Teddy is an excellent student, well liked by his classmates, but he is troubled because his mother has a terminal illness and life at home must be a struggle."

His third grade teacher wrote, "His mother's death has been hard on him. He tries to do his best, but his father doesn't show much interest and his home life will soon affect him if some steps aren't taken." Teddy's fourth grade teacher wrote, "Teddy is withdrawn and doesn't show much interest in school. He doesn't have many friends and sometimes sleeps in class."

By now of course, Mrs. Thompson realized what the real problem was. The problem with Teddy and the problem with herself. She was a mediocre teacher, taking the path of least resistance, and to be quite truthful, she was ashamed of herself. She decided to do better; to be the best teacher she could be! One day soon her students brought her Christmas presents, wrapped in beautiful ribbons and bright paper, all except for Teddy's. His present was poorly wrapped in a heavy, brown paper that he got from a grocery bag.

Mrs. Thompson, remembering the reports, took great pains to open it right in the middle of the other presents. Some of the children started to laugh when she found a rhinestone bracelet with some of the stones missing, and a bottle that was one quarter full of perfume. But, she cut off the children's laughter when she said how pretty the bracelet was. She took her own bracelet off and put Teddy's on her wrist. She then dabbed some of the perfume on her wrist.

Teddy Stoddard stayed after school that day just long enough to say, "Mrs. Thompson, today you smelled just like my Mom used to." After all the kids had left, Mrs. Thompson sat there and cried for at least an hour. On that very day, she quit teaching reading, and writing, and arithmetic. Instead, she began to teach children. She began to pursue excellence!

Mrs. Thompson began to pay particular attention to Teddy. The more she worked with him, the more his mind seemed to come alive. The more she encouraged him, the faster he responded. By the end of the year, Teddy had become one of the smartest kids in the class.

A year later, she found a note under her door, from Teddy, telling her that she was still the best teacher he ever had in his whole life.

Six years went by before Mrs. Thompson got another note from Teddy. He wrote her that he had finished high school, third in his class, and she was still the best teacher he ever had in his whole life.

Four years after that, she got another letter, saying that while things had been tough at times, he'd stayed in school, he'd stuck with it, and would soon graduate from college with honors. He assured Mrs. Thompson that she was still the best and favorite teacher he ever had in his whole life.

Then four more years passed and yet another letter came. This time he explained that after he got his bachelor's degree, he decided to go a little further. The letter explained that she was still the best and favorite teacher he ever had. But now his name was a little longer —the letter was signed, Theodore F. Stoddard, M.D.

The story doesn't end there. You see, there was yet another letter that spring. Teddy said he'd met this girl and was going to be married. He explained that his father had died a couple of years ago and he was wondering if Mrs. Thompson might agree to sit in the place at the wedding that was usually reserved for the mother of the groom. Of course, Mrs. Thompson did. And guess what? She wore that bracelet, the one with several rhinestones missing. And she made sure she was wearing the perfume that Teddy remembered his mother wearing on their last Christmas together. They hugged each, and Dr. Stoddard whispered in Mrs. Thompson's ear, "Thank you, Mrs. Thompson, for believing in me. Thank you so much for making me feel important and showing me that I could make a difference."

Mrs. Thompson, with tears in her eyes, whispered back. She said, "Teddy, you have it all wrong. You were the one who taught me that I could make a difference. I didn't know how to teach until I met you."

Sometimes the students become the teachers!

To all the teachers … trainers … educators … who have become disillusioned or been hurt … we need you! Our world needs you. Like the swords of Jason and his comrades, you've been through the fire. You may feel like you've been forged in the flames of despair, but you have a gift that we all need.

Our future depends on you! You, at one time, cared enough to care. Find some way to put your gifting to use. The army of Lefthanded Soldiers needs you!

Bonus Chapter Two
For Entrepreneurs and Dreamers

Recently, the infamous "they" released a list of the most dangerous places to live. City after city was listed, but I believe that they were way off. The most dangerous place to live is not a particular city. The most dangerous place to live … is in your comfort zone! For entrepreneurs and dreamers that is especially true. Some of the most creative, forward thinking, entrepreneurs and dreamers in history have been Lefthanded Soldiers! Walt Disney had multiple failures and yet, he kept on dreaming. Edison failed over a thousand times on the light bulb, but he changed history with his completed inventions. The list goes on and on. All around us there are new and fresh ideas looking for a receptive mind, waiting for someone to shake off the disappointments and challenges of the past and press forward. So, your right arm failed! Become a Lefthanded Soldier! Get back into the battle!

All dreams start with an idea. I've heard that thinking of new ideas is like shaving. If you don't do it every day, you're a bum. Just teasing, but you do need to begin to practice the old brainstorming concept EVERY DAY! Let the creative juices begin to flow. Let's get some new jelly on those convolutions. Let's stir up some imagination!

Everything begins with an idea. The chair you're sitting on. The CD you're listening to. The desk you're sitting at or the car you are riding in. They all started with an idea, and ideas birth dreams!

Ideas may begin to come slowly at first, but good ideas are like rabbits. You get a couple and pretty soon, you have a dozen!

Everyone of us have, at our disposal, a little over 18 billion brain cells. They are there just waiting, waiting for us to tell them what to do. The only limitations that exist in our lives are those we impose on ourselves. Think about this. Our brains do not know any limitations. Our minds were created to believe whatever we convince them to believe. So, sell the dream to yourself!

As Eleanor Roosevelt said, **"The future belongs to those who believe in the beauty of their dreams."**

The great Denis Waitley said, **"We've got to HAVE a dream if we are going to make a dream come true."**

And the great song writer Oscar Hammerstein said it this way, **"If you don't have a dream, how are you going to make a dream come true?"** They all agree that you've **GOT** to have a dream. So...DREAM AGAIN!

Having a dream, like having a vision, is forward thinking. Backward thinkers are sitting alone, like Jason, remembering "the good old days." If you don't have a dream; if you don't have a vision for your life, you are probably floundering. So let's stir you up! Let's begin to dream again! Let's stir up that entrepreneurial spirit again!

We need to live our life so that our tombstone will some day read, "No regrets." That requires having big dreams! When people say to me, "You live in a dream world!" I say, "Thank You!"

Albert Einstein said, "The important thing is to not stop questioning. Never lose a holy curiosity." That means we must think, we must dream, we must imagine what can be!

Ideas, dreams, imagination--they all help you to start thinking quickly on your feet. They all help you to adapt! Here's an example.

Your life is like a movie. You write the script. Is it a good script or a bad script? You are your own director. Do you give good, clear, thoughtful direction or do you just let things just "kinda' happen?" And, you are the star of your own life. How well do you play your role? Will it be a million dollar seller or a flop? Does your supporting cast draw from your strengths? What will be the reviews after the movie ends?

You are the master of your destiny, anything is within your reach. If you dream.

Let's have a dream session, or here's another term--let's visualize your life a little bit. Dreaming is just another form of concentration and focus. It's a method of programming the mind for success.

See your day before it starts. See your office or work area. Now, use your imagination a little bit. Smell the coffee. Hear the hum of the computer. Engage your senses. Walk through the appointments and see, hear and feel success! Start talking to yourself. Say some life changing affirmations! Shout like Jason did, "I'm ALIVE!" Swirl your sling around a few times!

Begin to feel confidence. Begin to feel joy. Thank God for good success!

Focus your energy. See each task completed. See people around you in a good mood. Laugh out loud. Come on now; this is fun! Dream. Have vision. Get great, inspired ideas. Imagine. This is a powerful principle!

The great Les Brown shares that there was a time that he was so broke that if he just walked by a bank, the alarms went off. But he learned that to have dreams was the first step toward making them realities.

You have to dream big to be big. The definition of impossible is: something nobody can do until somebody does it. But once it's done, it becomes possible to everyone. Roger Bannester dreamed of the four minute mile. It was impossible. Thousands had failed. But once he broke through the barrier, thousands of others have.

Sir Winston Churchill said, **"Courage is the capacity to go from failure to failure without losing enthusiasm."**

That means refusing to let go of your dream! That means learning to sling a stone at a hair and not miss. That means leaving the comfort zone of the "fig tree" and preparing for victory.

Heavyweight Champion George Foreman said, **"If you don't dream you might as well be dead."**

The scriptures say "Without a vision, or a dream, people perish."

Let's look at what Dr. Benjamin Isaiah Mays once said, **"It must be borne in mind that the tragedy of life does not lie in not reaching your goals, the tragedy lies in not having any goals to reach. It isn't a calamity to die with dreams unfulfilled, but it is a calamity not to dream. It is not a disaster to be unable to capture your ideals, but it is a disaster to have no ideals to capture. It is not a disgrace not to reach the stars, but it is a disgrace to have no stars to reach."**

A lot of people try once or twice, and if they fail, they quit. The truth is if at first you don't succeed, you are running about average.

Having a dream gives purpose and meaning to life. A dream gives us the reason to stretch ourselves, get out of our comfort zones, grab a "sling" and try something new.

A dream is bigger than your life. It will set the course of your life's work. You've got to have a dream! Wake up that entrepreneurial spirit! Refuse to accept failure. Become a Lefthanded Soldier.

Bonus Chapter Three
For Network Marketers and Direct Sales Professionals

Let's go ahead and admit it. The "all too familiar" battle cry of some past network marketers and direct sales professionals is, "I'll never, ever, ever do network marketing or anything like it again!" I know exactly how they feel. I've felt that way before. To me, MLM had become a four letter word! It's unfortunate, but true, a lot of people have been beaten up, bruised, and battered by network marketing. They cared enough to fight, but they were wounded, and like Jason, many of them have "retired" to sit under the proverbial fig tree. They grew "bitter," not "better." But like Benjamin, I believe there is still hope. Losing the battle does not mean we have to lose the war! Being wounded does not mean you are a failure. I'm not here to curse the darkness, I'm here to turn on the light. This chapter covers some very serious issues. We're going to talk about the facts! There **are** "ponsey schemes" out there. There **are** pyramid schemes out there. There **are** scams in the world. But, you can't have a counterfeit unless you have an original. Thank God for the real thing!

It's important to be honest enough to admit that there are issues out there in the Network Marketing profession. I train a lot for the industry, so I know whereof I speak. But, before we tackle them let's laugh at ourselves a little bit.

Laughter is a good medicine! Network marketing has been called a lot of things over the years: MLM, direct sales, interactive distribution, affiliate marketing, person to person marketing, and relationship marketing.

It's also been called a lot of things that I can't repeat publicly. Some people, have dubbed **"NETWORK"** marketing as **"NIT-WIT"** marketing. Nit-wit marketing, un-fit marketing, mis-fit marketing, been-bit marketing, took-a-hit marketing, and it's-the-pits marketing!

Let's talk about the top ten signs that will justify your new *network* marketing company might be dubbed *nit-wit* marketing.

(drum roll please)

Number ten, you are frisked and asked to go through a metal detector at your first opportunity meeting.

Number nine, your upline's phone was disconnected during your first three way call.

Number eight, the president of your new MLM company was escorted in by three body guards. They were all named Guido, and they all had an odd shaped lump under their arms.

Number seven, your company asked you to tape a success testimony, ten minutes after joining.

Number six, you were told to enlarge your garage because you would need the space to store products!

Number five, you were told that all real builders begin by ordering sixty-five thousand dollars worth of product immediately!

Number four, your first bonus check was four dollars and twenty-five cents. It was four weeks late. And it was so hot that it burst into spontaneous combustion, and bounced three times when it hit the ground!

Number three, your company-supplied leads are pages torn out of the local phone book!

Number two, you noticed that the three new men at the opportunity meeting all have "Sixty Minute" logos on their notebooks!

And the number one sign that your Network Marketing company might be dubbed a nit-wit marketing company is that an order from the attorney general with the words "cease and desist" at the top is included free with every new distributor kit.

Go ahead and admit it! Some of those hit way too close to home to laugh at too hard!

Nit-wit marketing! Sometimes we have deserved that!

It is true. There are some nit-wit marketing companies out there disguised as network marketing companies. There are those out there that say (with a straight face) they can sell you a product that will "make your hair grow, make your legs smooth, make your sex life wonderful, and make your weight fall off--all simultaneously." And, at the same time they can make you rich beyond your wildest dreams, without you doing one solitary thing!

Listen my friend. To use common language, "It ain't always the truth! What's on the label ain't always in the bottle."

I can tell you personally that there's been more than one check come late, and then bounce. There's been more than one company fail. There's been more than one company that changed their marketing plan every time the president had a "bright idea!" There's been more than one time that a "unilevel" turned into a "binary", which turned into a 'stair step break away", which turned into an "Australian Two Up" which turned into a **CATASTROPHE**!

Has anybody been there besides me? Has anybody else "been there, done that?" "Why in the world did I ever look at this? All I ever really needed was a *'real'* job."

And because we sometimes get knocked to our knees--get wounded--our human nature is that it is always a little bit harder to get up and try again the next time.

Unfortunately, sometimes you get "beat up" again the second time. And when somebody comes to you with a third opportunity, **you don't even want to listen to them!**

But after a while, because you really want to win, you decide to try again. At first, you have a little success and you start making good money. You finally think your future is secure. And then, it suddenly all craters because somebody at the top made a stupid decision and gross mismanagement knocks you down again!

Then, when somebody else sends you an email about an opportunity, you want to put a hammer through your computer screen! You don't want to see another opportunity, or as I sometimes call them, another *"sloportunity"*.

Does anybody understand what I'm talking about? You see, sometimes we don't want to admit these things. We're embarrassed! But we have to understand that if people like us, who have been in the industry, sometimes see network marketing in this light, how in the world must "outsiders" look at us?

But I believe we can still be winners.

There is hope!

Why did you get involved in network marketing in the first place? Did you want to be different? Did you get tired of somebody telling you how much you're worth? Did you get tired of somebody putting you in a box because of your gender, because of the color of your skin, because of your economic background, because of your past? Are you tired of people putting judgmental qualifications on you?

When you first saw Network Marketing you said to yourself , "Here's a world where everybody dreams! Here's a world where I can go out and be anything I want, do anything I want, and have anything I want!" Isn't that why you got involved? All the restraints are gone. Network marketing levels the playing field. It's truly an equal opportunity. Everybody can win!

Some of you have the potential to be the greatest network marketers in the world! But you are sitting "on the sidelines" because you got wounded in battle. You can be a Lefthanded Soldier. You can get back in the battle again. It may not be like it was. It may be different than it was. You can be the hero out leading the army again!

To all of the leaders that are reading this, I want you to be an encourager, not a discourager. Stop looking down on those who have been hurt and disappointed. Quit looking at them as dead meat. Quit looking at people as dollar signs. Look at their lives and go make a difference in their lives. If you'll make a difference in their lives, and they pass it on and they pass it on, and they pass it on, everyone will be better for it!

That's the power of duplication! That's what builds network marketing teams! Built the right way, it's built on relationships. Then, it doesn't matter what comes against you, you'll stand. If company problems come, you'll stand. If there is trouble with one of the products, you'll stand. If adversity hits, you'll stand. (You are a stud, not a dud or a studette, not a dudette!) You are a winner, not a whiner.

It works, folks, it works! Quit building checks and start building lives and your team will grow! And that will affect your financial future.

Bonus Chapter Four
For Ministers and Spiritual Leaders

Over the years I've had the privilege of speaking in
numerous churches.

I've seen hundreds of seemingly overworked and underpaid
ministers and their staff give of their lives until they were
completely empty. They had nothing left to give. Therein
lies the problem. Men do not have a limitless resource of
ANYTHING. Even Christ felt virtue go out from him when
he ministered. His example was to pull away and spend
time with His Father. Living as a man he needed to
replenish himself. He knew that if he did not "replenish" he
would "diminish!" We are no different.

You may have all the right reasons for "giving out" … but,
without the practical practices of "taking in" you will
ultimately have a diminished capacity to minister. This
opens the door to fatigue. This opens the door to failure.

Over the years great spiritual leaders have failed. Some
people automatically start screaming "HYPOCRICY!" In

most cases this is overly harsh, unfair and judgmental. Why do so many of the leaders then fail? Let's remember Jason's injury. The most exposed part of his body was wounded. It was that way in the entire army. What is exposed the most suffers the most wounds. Ministers and spiritual leaders put their lives out front and are exposed more than the rest of the "Body." Continual demands on their time often cause a breach in the family. While constantly comforting others they often have no one to confide in. This isolation ... combined with the overwhelming expectations ... combined with continued exposure often leads to wounds that others don't even know about until it's too late. Their shield of faith comes down. They are attacked. They are wounded in battle. And, like Jason, they are often dismissed from the army. Many great "soldiers in the army of God" are sitting under the proverbial fig tree somewhere. Wounded. Hurting. Disappointed. Angry. Bitter ... not better. All because they cared enough to fight!

They feel condemned to a life of "what-ifs." Condemned is the root word for condemnation. Please permit me to remind you of the scripture that says:

There is therefore now no condemnation to them which are in Christ Jesus, who walk not after the flesh, but after the Spirit. **Romans 8:1**

Let me speak directly to you, wounded warrior of the cross. Condemnation and guilt may come from other men, but it is not from God. Yes, you have been hurt. Yes, others may have been hurt in the process. But the army needs you! Become a Lefthanded Soldier!

Let me share a story that you need to hear. It's childlike in it's simplicity, but extremely prolific.

Butch and Sissy were nine year-old twins. They lived with their grandma on a little twelve-acre country farm.

While playing in the field one day, Sissy, who was extremely precocious swung her braided, bright red hair over her shoulder and dared Butch to throw a rock at Grandma's favorite goose who was nearby. Never one to back down from his sister's "dare", he playfully picked up a rock and chunked it in the direction of the goose. He was horrified when the heavy rock hit the goose in the head and the goose fell over dead! They stared at each other in disbelief and quickly grabbed the goose's body, took it behind the barn and buried it in a hole big enough for a horse. Then they went about their business trying to act as though nothing had happened.

It wasn't long until Grandma came out looking for her goose. It was her absolute favorite animal. When she could not find it she asked the children about it, and of course, they acted innocent. After checking with the neighbors and walking the entire property, Grandma realized that her goose was gone. It broke her heart and she literally took ill and went to bed for several days.

One day after the brief illness, Grandma decided that she needed to go into town and buy some groceries. Before she left, she called Butch and Sissy into the front room and gave them some chores to do. She told Butch to make all of the beds and told Sissy to clean the kitchen and wash the dishes. After she left, Butch went in and started his chores, but Sissy just went into the kitchen and stared at the mess and all the dishes in the sink. She devised a plan. She walked into the bedroom where Butch was and said, "Butch, go in there and do those dishes for me."

And of course he said, "No way!"

She said, "You better do the dishes for me or…"

"Or what?" Butch replied.

Then Butch heard the words that he would soon learn to dread, "Remember the goose!"

Butch said, "What about the goose?"

And Sissy said, "If you don't do the dishes for me, I'll tell Grandma that you killed her goose." And a brand new way of life was born. Everyday Butch heard Sissy say over and over again "Remember the goose!" He already felt bad enough for killing the goose in the first place, but this continual reminder was more than he could bare. Day in and day out, "Remember the goose!"

Several months later after Sissy had gone to bed, Grandma was in her rocking chair beside the fireplace darning a sock. Butch was lying on the floor. Grandma kept watching him, because he was very quiet and solemn. After a while she saw a small tear role down his cheek. Grandma spoke to him and asked him what was the matter. He just brushed her off and told her he was okay. After a few more minutes passed she noticed more tears. She asked him to come to her and Butch crawled up in his Grandma's lap and the tears flowed freely.

Finally, Butch looked up at his Grandmother and asked, "Grandma, do you love me?"

Grandma replied, "Of course, I love you."

Butch blurted out, "Grandma, I'm so sorry... I... I killed your goose!"

After what seemed like an eternity, Grandma looked him in the eye and said, "I know Butch. I found the bloody rock , found the grave, and I've heard Sissy taunting you."

Butch couldn't believe it. He said, "Grandma why didn't you tell me that you knew? Sissy's been driving me crazy!"

Grandma said, "Because I loved you enough for you to make the decision to come tell me."

The next day after Grandma went to the store for groceries, Sissy came into Butch's room, squinted her eyes and said, "Butch, go do my dishes for me!"

Butch just smiled. Sissy blurted out, "Remember the goose!" Butch just smiled. Sissy tossed her hair and once again in a high pitched voice shouted, "Remember the goose!"

Butch looked her in the eye and said, "I've already told Grandma… She forgave me… and she loves me anyway!"

And Sissy's perpetual voice of condemnation was silenced once and for all.

When you fail, it's good to know that God has already forgiven you. He's just waiting for you to own up to it.

When you do, the perpetual voices of condemnation we so often hear are silenced. Now, forgive yourself, and tell your accusers that you intend to get up, look up and some day go up!

There is room in the army for you! The army needs leaders with your experience. Become a Lefthanded Soldier. Learn to sling stones at a hair and not miss.

Bonus Chapter Five
For Volunteers and Public Servants

Years and years ago, a humble monk was traveling on a mountain road. As fate would have it, the traveling monk came across the path of a hungry traveler and decided to help him. The old, but wise, monk only had a few possessions. And yet, without hesitation, he opened a small burlap pouch that was hanging from his belt. The monk reached inside the pouch, looked at the other man and smiled, took out a beautiful precious stone that was worth a small fortune, reached out and gave it to the man.

Several days before the old monk had discovered the stone laying partially hidden by some fallen leaves on the side of the road. And ... he was now giving it away. The other traveler was amazed. He scarcely could believe his good fortune!

He left without hesitation because in his heart he had already decided to sell the valuable stone as soon as possible. But then something amazing happened. Something wonderful. The man decided to return after only a few days. He brought the beautiful, valuable jeweled stone with him.

The man, after finding the monk, quickly reached out and placed the stone in the monk's hand. He wrapped both of his hands around those of the monk and said, "Sir, if you will, please give me something that I believe is much more precious, much more valuable than this stone. He intently gazed into the eyes of the monk. Then he said, "Sir, I want you to please give me whatever it is that is inside of you that made you willing to give this stone away."

There is nothing more admirable than a giving heart. Nelson Henderson once said, "The true meaning of life is to plant trees under whose shade you do not expect to sit." That's giving for the sake of giving. That is the heart of a volunteer and a public servant.

One of the quickest ways for someone that is wounded and isolated to engage in life again is to volunteer, to begin to serve. Something amazing happens when you pour yourself into someone else's life. **YOUR LIFE** becomes fuller. Lefthanded Soldiers have experienced things that others have not. These valuable life lessons transcend all barriers. Why not let others benefit from your experience. You have gifts that I will never have. You can reach people I will never meet. But, like Jason, you must bury the ghost of the past and move on with life. Let's look at some lyrics I wrote.

**Bury The Ghost of the Past**
**Sometimes when I'm praying**
**A voice cries out to me**
**A lying ghost from the past**
**Stirs up memories**
**He tries to shroud my mind with doubt**
**Remember when, he asks**
**But beneath the Love of God**
**I'm gonna bury the ghost of the past**

Draw a line in the sand! Use your gift! Volunteer. Serve others. You'll be the better for it! What if Michelangelo had painted? What if Beethoven had refused to compose? What if Lance Armstrong refused to get back on his bicycle when he fell?

More importantly, what if you never choose to express your gift? Would it be like the movie "It's a Wonderful Life." Who is it that your gift would never touch? And who would it be that they never touch? And so on and so on . If you deny your passion, the world will be a different place. The Butterfly effect will take over and not only your life will be different but all creation would be affected.

Life is about unleashing the passion within. How does that happen? It begins when we serve others. Here's a story I once heard that will illustrate how "getting involved" will affect a lot more lives than your own.

One day a depressed and lonely man was walking home from work. His life was at a crossroads. Failure had led to frustration. His worry list was ever expanding. To make his frustration worse, HE WAS FREEZING! He slowly drudged ahead hanging his head to shelter it from the cold. He was used to looking down. This time it worked FOR him. He happened to see an old brown leather billfold with red lacing around it that someone must have lost in the street. He leaned over and picked it up, and as we all probably would do, he opened it up and looked inside to see if he could find some sort of identification so he could try and call the owner.

But unfortunately, the old billfold only had three crumpled one dollar bills in it and an extremely old crumpled up letter that looked like it had been in there for years. He was almost afraid to touch it. But curiosity spurred him on.

The old yellowed envelope was really worn out, and the only thing that was legible on it was a faded return address. So, he finally opened the letter, hoping to find some sort of clue. He was surprised at his interest. He may as well be interested in someone else's life; his was no prize! Then he saw the date on it--1924. Wow! That old letter had been written over sixty years ago. As he looked closer he saw that it had been written in a beautiful feminine handwriting on powder blue stationery. The paper had a little flower in the top left-hand corner.

As he began to scan the first page ever so carefully he realized that this was a "Dear John" letter. It told the recipient whose name looked like Michael that the she could not see him again. Her heart was broken, but, her mother had absolutely forbidden it. She went on to tell him that no matter what, she would always, always love him. She simply signed it, Hannah.

The man who found it was touched by the simple beauty of the letter. It felt good to see that at least somebody believed in love. As he thought about it, there was no way that the owner could be identified. No way in the world! He had nothing to go on except for the names, Michael and Hannah. He had a wild idea! Maybe if he called information, the operator could find a phone listing for the address on the envelope. It was worth a try.

So he called and said, "Operator," "I know this is a crazy request. I'm trying to find the owner of a billfold that I found. Is there any way, any way in the world that you can tell me if there is a phone number for an address that was on an envelope inside the billfold?"

She suggested that he speak with her supervisor, who hesitated for a moment then said, "Well, there is a phone listing at that address, but I can't give you the number."

"Oh no!'

But, she said, as a courtesy, she would call that number, explain the story and ask them if they wanted her to connect him.

So he waited a few minutes. It seemed like an eternity. The supervisor came back on the line. She said "I have a party who will speak with you."

This was getting exciting now. He asked the woman on the other end of the line if she knew anyone by the name of Hannah. The lady replied, "Oh! We bought this house from a family who had a daughter named Hannah. But that was 30 years ago!"

He asked her if she had any idea where that family was now?"

She said that Hannah had to place her mother in a nursing home years and years ago, but she suggested that if he got in touch with them they might be able to track down the daughter. So, she gave him the name of the nursing home and he called the number.

He found out that the mother had passed away some years before but after a lengthy search they found a phone number for where they thought the daughter might be living. So he tried that number. The woman who answered explained that Hannah herself was now living in a nursing home. So, the chase continued. This felt good. He was involved in life again!

He kept on plowing. Something was compelling him. He called the nursing home where Hannah was supposed to be living and the man who answered the phone told him, "Yes, Hannah was staying there."

Even though it was already 10 p.m, he asked if he could come by to see her. "Well it's up to you; if you want to take a chance. She might still be in the activity room watching television."

So, he thanked him and drove over to the nursing home. The nurse on duty and a security guard greeted him at the door. They all went up to the third floor and they did find Hannah in the day room.

Now Hannah was a sweet lady with silver blue hair who still had a warm smile and a twinkle in her eye. He told her about finding the wallet and showed her the letter.

The second she saw the powder blue paper with that little flower on the left, Hannah took a deep breath and said, "Young man, this letter was the last contact I ever had with Michael." She looked far, far away for a moment as tears came to her eyes, and then she said softly, "I loved him very much. But, I was only sixteen years old at the time and my mother felt I was too young. He was so handsome." Michael Goldstein was a wonderful person. If you should find him, tell him I think of him often. And," she hesitated for a moment, almost biting her lip, "tell him I still love him." She said smiling as tears began to well up in her eyes, "I never did marry. I guess no one ever matched up to Michael."

So the man thanked Hannah and said goodbye. He took the elevator to the first floor and as he stood by the door, the guard there asked, "Was the old lady able to help you?" He told him she had given him a lead. "At least I have a last name now. I'd sure love to find the owner of this billfold."

He took it out to show the guard. It was just a simple brown leather case with red lacing on the side. When the guard saw it, he said, "Hey, wait a minute! That's Mr. Goldstein's wallet. I'd know it anywhere with that right red lacing. He's always losing that wallet. I must have found it in the halls at least a dozen times."

"Who's Mr. Goldstein?" He asked as his hand began to shake.

"He's one of the old timers on the 8th floor. That's Mike Goldstein's wallet for sure. He must have lost it on one of his walks."

So he thanked the guard and quickly ran back to the nurse's office. He told her what the guard had said. He went back to the elevator praying that Mr. Goldstein would still be up. On the eighth floor, the floor nurse said, "I think he's still in the activity room. He likes to read at night. He's a darling old man." We went to the only room that had any lights on and there was a man reading a book.

The nurse went over to him and asked if he had lost his wallet. Mr. Goldstein looked up with surprise, put his hand in his back pocket and said, "Oh, it is missing!"

This nice man found a billfold and we wondered if it could be yours?" The man handed it to Mr. Goldstein and the second he saw it, he smiled with relief and said, "Yes, that's it! It must have dropped out of my pocket this afternoon. I want to give you a reward."

"No, thank you," he said. But he said, "I have to tell you something. I read the letter in the hopes of finding out who owned the wallet."

The smile on his face suddenly disappeared. "You read that letter?"

"Not only did I read it, I think I know where Hannah is." Mr. Goldstein suddenly grew pale.

"Hannah? You know where she is? How is she? Is she still as pretty as she was? Please, please tell me," he begged.

"She's fine--just as pretty as when you knew her." He said softly. The old man smiled with anticipation and asked, "Could you tell me where she is? I want to call her tomorrow." He grabbed my hand and said, "You know something, mister, I was so in love with that girl that when that letter came, my life literally ended. I never married. I guess I've always loved her."

"Mr. Goldstein," he said, "Come with me." We took the elevator down to the third floor. The hallways were darkened and only one or two little night-lights lit our way to the day room where Hannah was sitting alone watching the television.

The nurse walked over to her. "Hannah," she said softly, pointing to Michael, who was waiting with me in the doorway. "Do you know this man?" She adjusted her glasses, looked for a moment, but didn't say a word.

Michael said softly, almost in a whisper, "Hannah, it's Michael. Do you remember me?"

She gasped, "Michael! I don't believe it! Michael! It's you! My Michael!" He walked slowly towards her and they embraced. The nurse and the man who found the wallet left with tears streaming down their faces.

About three weeks later the same man got a call at his office from the nursing home. "Can you break away on Sunday to attend a wedding?" asked the nurse from the nursing home. "Michael and Hannah are going to tie the knot!"

It was a beautiful wedding with all the people at the nursing home dressed up to join in the celebration. Hannah wore a light beige dress and looked beautiful. Michael wore a dark blue suit and stood tall. They made that stranger their best man. The hospital gave them their own room and if you ever wanted to see a 76-year-old bride and a 79-year-old groom acting like two teenagers, you had to see this couple. A perfect ending for a love affair that had lasted nearly 60 years.

All of this happened because somebody put his own hurts aside, and got involved. He volunteered his time. He served someone else, and his life changed forever.

If you are down, if you are despondent, if your are depressed, volunteer to serve others. Put your hurts behind you and become a Lefthanded Soldier! Learn to serve in an army of volunteers and public servants that fill thousands of needs in millions of lives…every day.

About The Author

Gary Eby is an International Trainer and Sales Strategist. He has been given a dynamic gift to teach, train, motivate, and inspire.

Our generation is looking for leaders. Gary Eby is a leader. He has a God-given ability to communicate deep truths in a clear and easily understandable style. His message will lead you on a power-packed adventure that is often filled with laughter and practical illustrations.

Gary's gift has made room for him in meetings and teaching seminars all over the United States. He has also spoken in England, Japan and Brazil.

Having come from a diverse background, including the United States Marine Corps and as an international speaker, Gary's lifestyle mission statement includes the philosophy of "vision, integrity and diligence."

Gary has worked in the Direct Sales and Network Marketing Industries both at the corporate level and as a distributor. He has written and produced numerous videos, interactive CD's and various training materials for these industries through one of his companies, Digitech Seven Productions. This distinctive background gives him a unique insight into the aspirations of both the corporate officers and field producers.

Not only is Gary a sought-after speaker, but he is also an author and songwriter, having written numerous songs that have been recorded and performed worldwide on television, radio, and concert stages. Gary also conducts songwriting seminars through his publishing company, Bloodwine Publishing.

Winning is not an event. Winning is a way of life. It's a lifestyle! Society teaches us to lose. And sometimes we even see ourselves as losers! But I believe you can be a winner! I want to teach you to change the way you think. Think like a winner! Change the way you talk! Talk like a winner! Change the way you believe. Believe like a winner!

In this video you'll learn how to win! You'll learn how to overcome adversity. You'll learn to have a winning attitude. You'll learn how to take the actions necessary to finish the journey. While watching this presentation you'll laugh ... you'll cry ... and you'll be reminded of great truths you may have left behind. I want you to win ... and win big!

Charting Your Course
By the Dream
In Your Heart

People often wonder about the future. What will it hold? Can we do anything about it? Is our destiny a random victim of the circumstances we encounter ... or, can we begin today to set in motion a series of events that will cause our future to align with our dreams?

The American Dream
A Declaration of Financial Independence

I believe that God in His infinite wisdom has planted the seed of greatness in every man and every woman. It is my mission to develop that seed inside of you until you grow into the champion that you were meant to be.

Has corporate America stolen the dream? Has your dream been replaced by despair and disgust? You can dream again ... You can make your Declaration of Financial Independence!

Coming Soon!

Coming Soon!

True Confessions
of a
Christian
Entrepreneur

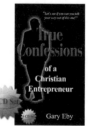

122

To order additional products by Gary Eby
please visit www.YourSuccessStore.com/Eby
or call (877) 929-0439

6 CD Set

**Power Principles
For
Peak Performance**

My 30 years of speaking has taught me that time is so important. This led me to invest over 3000 hours of my life to study and assemble complete trainings for people who understand the value of time ... and the value of instruction! So I developed 30 one hour strategies and skill sessions. A lifetime of accumulated knowledge.

These 30 one hour messages have now been condensed into 30 sessions that are about 10 -12 minutes each. These are compressed in time ... but not in powerful content! They will unlock your hidden power to succeed. Only the best of the best made the cut! Hundreds of practical illustrations and stories that will make you want to listen over and over again! In 30 days ... you can change your future!

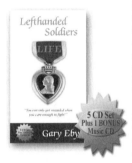

**5 CD Set
Plus 1 BONUS
Music CD**

Sometimes in life you get wounded. This series is dedicated to all of those who have been wounded in life ... whether physically, emotionally, spiritually, or financially and yet, against all odds, have risen from the devastation to become a champion! To some MLM has become a four letter word. This series helps you help those people!
It tells the difference between "Network Marketing" and "Nitwit Marketing" contains training, Interview, Audio Book and a Bonus Contemporary Christian Music CD! Designed especially for Network Marketers who want to build a team ...AND build lives!

New Book

It's a novel! It's life training! It's NOT JUST FOR NETWORK MARKETERS! Five BONUS Chapters! To order additional copies of the book Lefthanded Soldiers see quantity discounts below.
Retail $12.95

1-9	$ 9.00 ea	*www.YourSuccessStore.com*
10-24	$ 7.00 ea	*(877) 929-0439*
25-99	$4.50 ea	*(817) 442-8549*
100+	$3.00 ea	*FAX (817) 442-1390*

123

Gifts that Inspire and Tools to Build Your Business...

Excerpts from the Treasury of Quotes

*Jim's, Brian's, Zig's or Denis' booklets can be given as a stand-alone gift
or enclosed with a gift card or thank you note. They are the perfect
addition that will have a positive effect on the recipient and are sure to be
kept forever and not thrown away like a note or business card might be.
Perfect for customers, family and friends!*

Excellent for those of you involved with:

· **Real Estate**	· **Sales**
· **Mortgage**	· **Training**
· **Insurance**	· **Toastmasters**
· **Network Marketing**	· **Doctors/Dentists**
· **Chiropractors**	· **Educators/Coaches**

For mix and match pricing, see back page...

The Treasury of Quotes

*Features 365 quotes on 60 topics gathered over
40 plus years of wit and wisdom from Jim Rohn.
A must for your library!*
Burgundy hardback with gold foil lettering.
Retail $20 each
Special $12 each

Building Your Network Marketing Business

**The Hottest single CD ever created in the Network Marketing
Industry!**

Subjects include: Awakening to the Opportunity,
Profits are Better than Wages, The Magic of Part-
Time, The Set of the Sail, The Law of Averages, The
Law of Sowing & Reaping and more! Use for both
Training and Recruiting!

To order these products or other products go to www.jimrohn.com or
call 800-929-0434.

What Others Are Saying, cont.

"I've met Presidents, Senators, millionaires and thousands of people to whom I speak every year. But seldom have I met a person like Gary Eby. Gary's quiet wit explodes, whether on stage or on the page. His famous "Ebyisms" make you think, and his passion to change lives is contagious. When I listen to Gary teach, I've always got my Ipaq ready because I know I'll be collecting dozens of nuggets. His strength lies in his ability to effectively communicate life-challenging truths."

Harold Herring
President, Debt Free Army

"Gary Eby is Refreshing, Insightful, and Entertaining. His trainings are full of Passion, Energy, and Excitement! If you're the type of person who wants to be told how it is, then Gary is for you!"

Jerry "DRhino" Clark
Motivational Speaker and TV Show Host

"Having worked with some of the greatest speakers in the industry, I can say with no reservations that Gary is one of the most impactful speakers I've ever heard. If you need a speaker to light an inspirational fire in the room that will burn in the minds of your audience long after the event is finished – Gary is your man!"

Matt Morris
President and CEO, Success University

"I've shared the platform with Gary numerous times. His passion always comes through. Sometimes we speakers are guilty of leaving the room when 'we' are not speaking. Not when Gary Eby is on!"

Johnny Wimbrey
Motivational Speaker and
Author of "From The Hood, To Doing Good"

"Last year we had an awesome meeting in Florence, South Carolina at the Civic Center. We had great athletes speaking there like Brian Holloway, Rayfield Wright and William 'Refrigerator' Perry. They had the Super Bowl rings ... but Gary Eby had the crowd!"

Evelyn Hobson
Network Marketing Consultant

"Gary has spoken for us at several National Conventions, both in the United States and Japan. Even with a translator his humor and joy came through. Gary is rare in that he has both "passion" and "com-passion." He really cares about the little guy!"

Rick Bailey
CEO of The Right Solution

"Gary has an almost uncanny ability to motivate, inspire, and lead you and your team to greater levels of performance and endurance, while simultaneously keeping them on the edge of their seat. Lefthanded Soldiers continues this heritage in spades and is a must read for anyone wanting to maximize their competitive advantages in today's marketplace."

Rick & Michelle Teague
Independent Consultants &
Executive National Vice Presidents
Arbonne International